100%
Vegetarian

MICROWAVE DESI KHANA

Tarla Dalal

S&C

SANJAY & CO.
BOMBAY

Second Printing 2001
Copyright © Sanjay & Company
ISBN No. 81-86469-37-0

Price : Rs. 95/-

Published & Distributed by:
SANJAY & COMPANY,
353/A-1, Shah & Nahar Industrial Estate,
Dhanraj Mill Compound, Lower Parel (W),
Mumbai-400 013. Tel: (91-22) 496 8068.
Fax: (91-22) 496 5876. Email: sanjay@tarladalal.com

Recipe Research And Production Design	**Photography**
PINKY DIXIT	VINAY MAHIDHAR
ARATI KAMAT	
JYOTI JAIN	**Food Styling**
	NITIN TANDON
Designed by	**Printed by**
S. KISHOR	JUPITER PRINTS, Mumbai.

OTHER BOOKS BY TARLA DALAL

INDIAN COOKING

Tava Cooking
Rotis & Subzis
Desi Khana
The Complete Gujarati
Cook Book
Mithai
Chaat

WESTERN COOKING

The Chocolate Cook Book
Eggless Desserts
Mocktails & Snacks
Soups & Salads
Mexican Cooking
Easy Gourmet Cooking
The Complete Italian
Cook Book

HEALTH COOKING

Low Calorie Healthy Cooking
Eat Your Way To Good Health

EASTERN COOKING

Chinese Cooking
Thai Cooking

GENERAL COOKING

Exciting Vegetarian Cooking
Party Cooking
Microwave Cooking
Quick & Easy Vegetarian
Cooking
Saatvik Khana
Mixer Cook Book
The Pleasures of Vegetarian
Cooking
The Delights of Vegetarian
Cooking
The Joys of Vegetarian Cooking
Cooking With Kids

MINI SERIES

A New World Of Idlis & Dosas
Cooking Under 10 Minutes
Pizzas And Pasta
Fun Food For Children
Roz Ka Khana

INTRODUCTION

The microwave oven has revolutionized the way we cook. The fast cooking, fast clean up qualities of microwave cooking fit right into the life styles of today's busy homemakers. Little wonder then that microwave ovens have now earned a place in thousands of Indian homes.

What is it that makes microwave cooking so special? First, of course, is the speed with which it heats and cooks food. So you cut down on cooking time and seal in the freshness as well.

Microwave cooking also tends to be low-fat and hence is good for calorie watchers. Finally, as you will learn from your own experience as well as from the handy tips given in this book, the microwave oven provides a host of new shortcuts and problem solvers for chores such as roasting papads, blanching and steaming vegetables, making popcorn etc. Soggy and soft namkeens and nuts become crisp on microwaving for only a minute.

You will be surprised at the numbers of recipes on Indian food that can be made in the microwave. This book takes you on a culinary tour through every course of an Indian meal. **To test the recipes in this book, I have used a 20 litre microwave with an 800 watt output. Please refer to your own microwave manual as cooking times may vary with each individual microwave.**

The book includes Jhatpat Naashtas like Tandoori Aloo, Khaman Dhoklas ; Swadisht Subziyan like Vatana nu Oondhiyu, Vegetable Makhanwala, Methi Mutter Malai ; One Dish Meals like Ek Top Na Daal Bhaat as well as Desi Mithai like Sitafal Firni. All are modified in such a way that they provide the modern homemaker a guide to effortless cooking.

This book provides you recipes which make your everyday meals more flavoured as well as low in calories.

Welcome to cooking Indian food the modern way, quickly and efficiently!

4

WHAT ARE MICROWAVES?

A lot of people have asked me whether microwave cooking is harmful for health. Let me solve this query as simply as possible. There are two types of rays, firstly IONIZING RAYS (like x-rays, gamma rays as also cosmic rays which being short, build up in the body and are harmful), and secondly NON-IONIZING RAYS which do not build up in the body and hence are non-hazardous. Sunlight, radio and television rays and microwaves are all non-ionizing rays.

HOW DOES A MICROWAVE OPERATE?

Microwaves are high-frequency electromagnetic waves which release energy to food to cook or reheat without changing either the form or the colour.

You can use your microwave oven to :
- Defrost
- Reheat
- Cook

COOKING PRINCIPLE

1. The microwaves generated by the magnetron tube are distributed uniformly as the food rotates on the glass plate. The food is thus cooked evenly.
2. The microwaves are absorbed by the food up to a depth of about 25 mm. (1"). Cooking then continues as the heat is distributed within the food.

3. Cooking times vary according to the following properties of the food :
   a. Quantity and density
   b. Water content
   c. Initial temperature (refrigerated or not)

As the centre of the food is cooked by heat distribution, cooking continues even when you have taken the food out of the oven. **Standing times** specified in recipes must therefore be respected to ensure both even cooking of the food right to the centre as also achieving the same temperature throughout the food.

MICROWAVE COOKING TECHNIQUES

Microwave cooking isn't really so different from traditional cooking and the factors that affect the cooking time for conventional methods of cooking also apply here. However, the following factors need to be borne in mind.

1. Microwave cooking time is greatly affected by the **QUANTITY** of food cooked. This means that the cooking time increases if any ingredient is added to the recipe.
2. The **SIZE** of the pieces of food also affects the cooking time. Small cubes of potato cook more quickly and evenly than large ones. Also, thinner slices cook faster than thick ones.
3. Appropriate **ARRANGEMENT** of food in your microwave can help the food cook better. Arrange the thicker, slower cooking pieces towards the outside edge. The food in the centre is generally the last to cook.

6

4. Using proper **UTENSILS** makes a difference too. Food tends to cook more evenly in round dishes than other shapes, and food spread out in a shallow dish will cook faster than the same food placed in a narrow deep dish.

MICROWAVE COOKWARE

To cook food in the microwave oven, the microwaves must be able to penetrate the food without being reflected or absorbed by the dish used.

Care must therefore be taken when choosing the cookware. If the cookware is marked microwave-safe, you do not need to worry.

The following table lists various types of cookware and indicates whether and how they should be used in a microwave oven.

To test if your glass / china / earthenware / plastic ware is microwavable, place it in a microwave oven filled with a cup of cold tap water. Microwave on HIGH for 1 minute. If the water is warm and the container is cool, the container can be used.

COOKWARE	MICROWAVE SAFE	COMMENTS
Aluminum foil	Avoid	Can be used with care in small quantities to protect areas against overcooking. Sparks can occur if the foil is too close to the oven wall or if too much foil is used.
China and earthenware	✓	Porcelain, pottery, glazed earthenware and bone china are usually suitable **unless** decorated with a **metal trim.**
Glassware		
a. Oven-to-table ware	✓	Can be used **unless** decorated with a **metal trim.**
b. Fine glassware	✓	Can be used to warm foods or liquids. Delicate glass may break or crack if heated suddenly.
c. Glass jars	✓	Must remove the lid. Suitable for warming only.
d. Bottles or containers with narrow necks	Avoid	If overheated, the container may explode as the pressure which builds up in the bottle cannot be let out through the narrow neck.

COOKWARE	MICROWAVE SAFE	COMMENTS
Metal		
Dishes, Spoons, skewers etc.	✖	May cause sparks or fire.
Paper		
a. Plates, cups, napkins, kitchen paper	✓	For short cooking times and warming. Also to absorb excess moisture.
b. Recycled paper	✖	May contain materials that can cause fire.
Plastic		
a. Containers and cups	✓	Only heat-resistant thermoplastic can be used. Other plastics may warp or discolour at high temperature. Do not use melamine plastic.
b. Cling film	✓	Can be used to retain moisture. Should not touch the food. Take care when removing the film as hot steam will escape.
Wax or grease-proof paper	✓	Can be used to retain moisture and prevent spattering.

COVERS

Covering a container in which the food is cooked helps to hold the steam, keeps the food moist, distributes the heat more evenly and contains splatters and spillage.

Here are a few handy hints to help you choose the best cover for your container.

1. Close fitting lids of microwave-safe material may be used.

2. Plastic wraps though more versatile may melt if they touch hot food. Hence always ensure that the plastic wrap you are using is microwave-safe.

3. When you want to retain a minimal amount steam in the dish, cover the food loosely with wax paper or damp cloth.

4. A paper napkin when used as a cover absorbs the grease or excess moisture.

5. Rice and dals are cooked uncovered to prevent spillage of water due to boiling over.

6. Do not use air-tight or vacuum-sealed bottles, jars or containers as microwaving might cause increase of pressure inside them and in turn may cause them to explode.

"DONENESS" AND STANDING TIME

Some recipes call for standing / resting time to complete cooking and to allow the heat to distribute evenly throughout the food. For this, you may place the container without removing the lid on a flat surface or simply leave it in the microwave with the power off. It is easy to overcook foods in a microwave oven, so if the food seems nearly done, let it complete its **resting** time and then check whether it is done. If it is still undercooked, you should microwave it further.

MODIFYING MICROWAVE RECIPES

Doubling or halving a microwave recipe requires careful consideration.

1. To double a recipe, you would have to increase the liquid content by 50% only and not double it as evaporation is slower. The cooking time also increases, so it is advisable to start with 50% more time.

2. When you reduce a recipe by half, keep the same sized dish but reduce the cooking time by half and then increase it as required.

CARING FOR YOUR MICROWAVE

1. Always keep your microwave oven clean and handle it gently. Do not bang the microwave doors when shutting them.

2. Do not cover the ventilation slots with cloth or paper. The cloth or paper may catch fire as hot air is evacuated from the oven.

3. **Never operate the oven when empty to avoid damage to the oven walls.**

4. **Do not use metal containers, non-microwaveable plastic containers, chinaware with metal rims and recycled paper.** Details given in section on Microwave cookware on pages 7 to 9.

5. For quick microwave clean-up, heat about 1/2 cup of water to boiling point. The steam will help any spills or stains to come off more easily.

6. If your microwave is damaged in some way and there is leakage of the microwaves, stop using it immediately and have it checked by a professional microwave serviceman.

MICROWAVE MAGIC

Given below are some handy tips and quick fixes that will make your daily cooking less of a chore.

a. **Dried Herbs (mint, basil, fenugreek, parsley)** : Just place one cup of the fresh herbs in a glass dish and microwave on HIGH for 3 minutes. Remove and crush them lightly. Store in an air-tight container.

b. **Popcorn** : Just place half a cup of popping corn in a large glass dish covered with a lid and microwave on HIGH for 3 minutes with 2 tablespoons of butter and salt to taste.

c. **Roasting** : Half a cup of cashewnuts or almonds when microwaved on HIGH for 1 minute and 30 seconds make crisper nuts. Papads and spices can be roasted by microwaving for only a minute.

d. **Blanching Almonds** : Just combine ½ cup of almonds with a quarter cup of water and microwave on HIGH for 3 minutes. Allow to stand for 2 minutes, drain and then peel the skins.

e. **Zero Fat Potato Wafers** : Slice the potatoes thinly, soak them in ice cold water for about 10 to 15 minutes, drain and pat dry on an absorbent cloth and microwave on HIGH, arranged in a single layer in a flat plate for 5 to 6 minutes or until crisp. Salt and spices can be sprinkled over later.

INDEX

DAL AUR CHAWAL

CHATPATE ACHAAR

DESI MITHAI

Please Note -

To test the recipes in this book, I have used a 20 litre microwave with an 800 watt output. Please refer to your own microwave manual as cooking times may vary marginally with each individual microwave.

JHATPAT NAASHTA

The magic of microwave cooking lies in the fact that so many snacks can be made quickly and effortlessly. Muthias, the traditional Gujarati steamed savoury, can be rustled up in a few minutes saving 80% of the cooking time. Moreover, the colour of the vegetables is retained making the snacks even more nutritious and eye-appealing. It is however not advisable to make the tempering ('tadka') in a microwave as it takes more time to do so. Hence, the conventional method for tempering has been used in these recipes.

BABY CORN HARA MASALA

Picture on page 17

Chunks of baby corn cooked in a spicy coriander paste.

Prep. time : 10 min.

❣

Cooking time : 6 min.

❣

Serves 2.

1 cup baby corn, cut into 4 lengthwise
1 teaspoon lemon juice
1 teaspoon sugar
2 tablespoons oil
salt to taste

To be ground into a paste
1 cup chopped coriander
12 mm. (½") piece ginger
2 cloves garlic
1 green chilli
1 onion, chopped
1 teaspoon cumin (jeera) seeds

For the garnish
1 tablespoon sliced tomatoes
4 lemon wedges

1. In a glass bowl, add the oil and the prepared paste. Microwave on HIGH for 1 minute.

Facing page: **Top-** Baby Corn Hara Masala, above
Bottom- Khaman Dhokla, page 30

2. Add the baby corn, salt and 2 tablespoons of water and mix well. Cover with a lid and microwave on HIGH for 6 minutes.

3. Add the lemon juice and sugar. Mix well.

▶ **Serve hot, garnished with the sliced tomatoes and lemon wedges.**

MOONG DAL KHANDVI

Picture on page 35

A delicious starter made with split yellow gram and curds and tempered with sesame seeds and mustard seeds.

Prep. time : 10 min.

❖

Cooking time : 6 min.

❖

Serves 2.

½ cup soaked moong dal (split yellow gram)

½ cup curds

1 teaspoon ginger-green chilli paste

¼ teaspoon turmeric (haldi) powder

¼ teaspoon asafoetida (hing)

salt to taste

For the tempering

1 teaspoon mustard (rai) seeds

1 teaspoon sesame (til) seeds

Facing page: Tandoori Aloo, page 21

¼ teaspoon asafoetida (hing)
2 tablespoons oil

For the garnish
2 tablespoons chopped coriander

1. Drain and grind the moong dal to a very fine paste in a food processor using 1 tablespoon of water.
2. Combine the moong dal paste, curds, ginger-green chilli paste, turmeric powder, asafoetida, salt and 3 tablespoons of water and mix very well in a glass bowl. Microwave on HIGH for 4 minutes, stirring in between after 2 minutes.
3. Spread the mixture thinly on the back of three 200 mm. (8") diameter thalis. Allow to cool for five minutes.
4. Cut the khandvi into 50 mm. (2") thick strips. Carefully roll up each strip.

How to proceed
1. For the tempering, heat the oil in a pan and add the mustard seeds.
2. When they crackle, add the sesame seeds and asafoetida and pour on top of the prepared khandvis.

▶ **Serve, garnished with the coriander.**

Handy Tip :
Soak the moong dal at least 3 to 4 hours before use. A quarter cup of raw moong dal will yield approximately ½ cup soaked moong dal.

TANDOORI ALOO

Picture on page 18

Baby potatoes tossed in a spicy mixture make a great cocktail snack.

Prep. time :
5 min.

❖

Cooking time :
9 min.

❖

Serves 2.

1 cup baby potatoes
1 tablespoon cream
¼ teaspoon kasuri methi
(dried fenugreek leaves)
1 tablespoon oil
salt to taste

To be ground into a paste

4 Kashmiri chillies
2 cloves garlic
12 mm. (½") piece ginger
2 teaspoons coriander-cumin seed
(dhania-jeera) powder

▶ 1. Wash the potatoes thoroughly, pierce them with a fork and place them all around the circumference of the microwave turntable. Place a glass of water in the centre to prevent the potatoes from getting wrinkled. Microwave on HIGH for 5 to 6 minutes until the potatoes are soft.

▶ 2. Heat the oil in a glass bowl, add the prepared paste and salt and mix well. Microwave on HIGH for 1 minute.

▶ 3. Add the potatoes, cream and kasuri methi and microwave on HIGH for 2 minutes.

▶ Serve hot.

PALAK METHI NA MUTHIA

These spinach and fenugreek dumplings make delicious tea-time treats.

Prep. time :
10 min.
❖
Cooking time :
10 min.
❖
Serves 4.

For the muthias

3 cups chopped spinach (palak)

1½ cups chopped fenugreek (methi) leaves

1 teaspoon green chilli-ginger paste

2 tablespoons whole wheat flour (gehun ka atta)

1 tablespoon Bengal gram flour (besan)

1 tablespoon semolina (rawa)

½ teaspoon cumin (jeera) seeds

a pinch soda bi-carb

2 teaspoons sugar

1 tablespoon lemon juice

1 tablespoon oil

salt to taste

oil for greasing

For the tempering

1 teaspoon sesame (til) seeds

¼ teaspoon asafoetida (hing)

1 tablespoon oil

For the muthias

1. Combine the spinach and fenugreek leaves with 1 teaspoon of salt and keep aside for about 5 minutes.
2. Squeeze out all the liquid and place the spinach and fenugreek leaves in a bowl.
3. Add all the remaining ingredients (other than for the tempering) and knead to a very soft dough adding 1 to 2 tablespoons of water if required.
4. Apply a little oil on your hands and divide the mixture into 4 equal portions. Shape each portion into a cylindrical roll approximately 150 mm. (6") length and 25 (1") in diameter .
5. Place 2 rolls in a greased shallow glass dish. Cover with a lid and microwave on HIGH for 3 minutes. Allow to stand for 1 minute.
6. Remove and keep aside. Repeat step 5 to steam 2 more rolls.
7. Cut into 12 mm. (½") slices and keep aside.

How to proceed

1. To prepare the tempering, heat the oil in a large pan and add the sesame seeds. When the seeds crackle, add the asafoetida.
2. Add the sliced muthias, toss well and stir over gentle heat for 2 to 3 minutes till they are lightly browned.

▶ Serve hot with green chutney.

Handy Tip :

To check if the muthias are done, insert a toothpick in the centre. If it comes out clean, the muthias are cooked.

SABUDANA KHICHADI

A delicious snack. Ideal for fasting.

Prep. time :
20 min.

❖

Cooking time :
4 min.

❖

Serves 4.

1 cup sago (sabudana)
½ cup roasted peanuts, crushed
2 medium potatoes, peeled and cut into cubes
½ teaspoon cumin (jeera) seeds
2 green chillies, slit
2 tablespoon oil
salt to taste

▶ 1. Wash the sago. Drain and keep aside for about 2 hours. If necessary sprinkle a little water to moisten the sago.

▶ 2. In a glass bowl, combine the oil, cumin seeds, green chillies and potatoes. Cover with a lid and microwave on HIGH for 2 minutes until the potatoes are tender.

▶ 3. Add the soaked sago, peanuts and salt and mix well. Cover with a lid and microwave on HIGH for 2 minutes.

▶ **Serve hot with green chutney or curds.**

CABBAGE STUFFED CAPSICUMS

An elegant snack of capsicums filled with a cabbage and Bengal gram flour mixture.

Prep. time : 10 min.

❖

Cooking time : 6 min.

❖

Serves 2.

2 medium sized capsicums
oil for greasing

For the filling
½ cup cabbage, grated
½ cup Bengal gram flour (besan)
2 teaspoons sugar
¼ teaspoon citric acid crystals
1 teaspoon green chilli-ginger paste
2 tablespoons chopped coriander
¾ teaspoon Eno's fruit salt
salt to taste

For the tempering
½ teaspoon mustard (rai) seeds
1 teaspoon sesame (til) seeds
¼ teaspoon asafoetida (hing)
2 tablespoons oil

1. Cut the capsicum into halves vertically. Remove the seeds carefully so as to retain the shape of the halves.

2. Mix all the ingredients for the filling except the fruit salt in a bowl with 4 tablespoons of water.
3. Add the fruit salt with 1 teaspoon of water and mix gently.
4. Fill each capsicum half with the filling.
5. Place the capsicum halves in a greased glass bowl. Cover with a lid and microwave on HIGH for 3 minutes.
6. Allow the capsicums to cool. Cut each capsicum half into thick strips.

How to proceed
1. Heat the oil in a large pan, add the mustard seeds and when they crackle, add the sesame seeds and asafoetida.
2. Add the capsicum pieces and sauté for 1 to 2 minutes, till they brown lightly.

▶ **Serve hot.**

MAKAI NI KHICHDI

A delicious Gujarati style snack.

Prep. time :
10 min.
❖
Cooking time :
6 min.
❖
Serves 4.

3 large sweet corncobs, grated
½ teaspoon mustard (rai) seeds
½ teaspoon cumin (jeera) seeds
¼ teaspoon asafoetida (hing)
1 green chilli, chopped
1 teaspoon sugar
juice of ½ lemon
1 teaspoon oil
salt to taste

For the garnish
2 tablespoons chopped coriander

▶ 1. In a glass bowl, combine the oil, mustard seeds, cumin seeds, asafoetida and green chilli and microwave on HIGH for 1 minute.

▶ 2. Add the grated corn, sugar, salt and 1 cup of water and microwave on HIGH for 5 minutes.

▶ 3. Add the lemon juice and mix well.

▶ 4. Garnish with the coriander and serve hot.

DOODHI MUTHIA

A steamed savoury made with doodhi (white pumpkin), 3 kinds of flours and fresh spices.

Prep. time :
10 to 15 min.

❖

Cooking time :
9 min.

❖

Serves 4 to 6.

For the muthias

2 cups white pumpkin (lauki), grated
1 onion, grated (optional)
1 cup whole wheat flour (gehun ka atta)
¾ cup semolina (rawa)
½ cup Bengal gram flour (besan)
2 tablespoons green chilli-ginger paste
½ teaspoon turmeric (haldi) powder
½ teaspoon garam masala
½ teaspoon cumin (jeera) seeds
½ teaspoon fennel (saunf) seeds
juice of 1½ lemons
2 tablespoons sugar
2 to 3 tablespoons chopped coriander
½ teaspoon soda bi-carb
½ teaspoon asafoetida (hing)
4 tablespoons oil
salt to taste

For the tempering

2 teaspoons mustard (rai) seeds
1 tablespoon sesame (til) seeds
½ teaspoon asafoetida (hing)
4 tablespoons oil

For the garnish

2 tablespoons chopped coriander

2 tablespoons grated coconut

For the muthias

▶ 1. Strain the liquid out of the grated pumpkin and onion, keeping the liquid aside to use if required to knead the dough.

▶ 2. Combine all the ingredients for the muthias in a bowl and knead into a very soft dough adding the strained vegetable liquid if required.

▶ 3. Using oiled palms, divide the mixture into 4 parts and roll out into cylindrical rolls approximately 200 mm. (8") long and 25 mm. (1") in diameter.

▶ 4. Place 2 cylindrical rolls in a greased shallow glass dish and cover with a lid.

▶ 5. Microwave on HIGH for 2 minutes. Allow it to stand for 1 minute.

▶ 6. Repeat steps 4 and 5 to make 2 more rolls.

▶ 7. Cool and slice into 20 mm. (¾") pieces and keep aside.

How to proceed

▶ 1. To prepare the tempering, heat the oil in a large pan and add the mustard seeds and sesame seeds. When they crackle, add the asafoetida.

▶ 2. Add the sliced muthias, toss well and stir over a medium flame for 2 to 3 minutes.

▶ 3. Garnish with the coriander and coconut.

▶ Serve hot with green chutney.

Handy Tip :
To check if the muthias are done, insert a toothpick in the centre. If it comes out clean, the muthias are cooked.

Variation :
You can use cabbage or fenugreek leaves instead of pumpkin.

KHAMAN DHOKLA

Picture on page 17

A traditional Gujarati snack, prepared in a jiffy.

Prep. time :
10 min.

❖

Cooking time :
6 min.

❖

Serves 4.

1 cup Bengal gram flour (besan)
1½ tablespoons fine semolina (rawa)
½ teaspoon citric acid crystals
3 teaspoons sugar
1 teaspoon green chilli-ginger paste
1½ teaspoons Eno's fruit salt
salt to taste

For the tempering
½ teaspoon mustard (rai) seeds
½ teaspoon sesame (til) seeds
2 green chillies, chopped

a pinch asafoetida (hing)
1 tablespoon oil

For the garnish
1 tablespoon chopped coriander
1 teaspoon chilli powder

1. Combine all the ingredients except the fruit salt in a bowl and make a batter using 1 cup of water.
2. Add the fruit salt. Sprinkle a little water over the fruit salt and mix well.
3. Pour half the batter into a greased 150 mm. (6") diameter microwaveable container and cover with a plastic wrap.
4. Microwave on HIGH for 2 minutes. Allow to stand for 1 minute.
5. Repeat with the remaining batter to make 1 more tray of dhoklas. Keep aside.

How to proceed
1. To prepare the tempering, heat the oil in a small pan and add the mustard seeds. When they crackle, add the sesame seeds, green chilli and asafoetida and remove from the fire. Add 1 tablespoon of water and pour the mixture over the steamed dhoklas.
2. Garnish with the coriander and sprinkle with the chilli powder.
3. Cut into pieces and serve with green chutney.

PANEER TIKKA

Cottage cheese and capsicum marinated in tandoori spices.

Prep. time :
25 min.

✿

Cooking time :
3 min.

✿

Serves 4.

2 cups paneer, cut into
50 mm. (2") cubes

½ cup capsicum, cut into
50 mm. (2") pieces

½ cup thick curds

1 teaspoon ginger paste

1 teaspoon garlic paste

2 teaspoons chilli powder

½ teaspoon kasuri methi
(dried fenugreek leaves)

½ teaspoon garam masala

2 tablespoons chopped coriander

1 teaspoon chaat masala

1 tablespoon oil

salt to taste

▶ 1. Combine the curds, ginger paste, garlic paste, chilli powder, kasuri methi, garam masala, coriander, oil and salt and mix well to prepare a marinade.

▶ 2. Add the paneer and capsicum to it and keep aside for 15 minutes.

▶ 3. Arrange the marinated paneer and capsicum pieces in a shallow glass dish and microwave on HIGH for 3 minutes.

▶ **Serve hot, sprinkled with the chaat masala.**

SWAADISHT SUBZIYAN

One always faces great difficulty trying to source recipes of subzis that are quick and easy to make. Once you cook these vegetables in the microwave, you will never enjoy it any other way. These mouth-watering delicacies can not only be rustled in minutes, they also retain their colour thus making them even more eye-appealing.

PANEER PALAK

Cubes of cottage cheese simmered in a spinach gravy.

Prep. time : 5 min.

❖

Cooking time : 6 min.

❖

Serves 2.

4 cups spinach (palak), chopped
½ cup paneer, cut into
25 mm. (1") cubes

1 onion, chopped
12 mm. (½") piece ginger,
finely chopped

2 green chillies, finely chopped
1 teaspoon coriander (dhania) powder
¼ teaspoon turmeric (haldi) powder
½ teaspoon garam masala
2 tablespoons cream
3 tablespoons oil
salt to taste

▶ 1. Place the chopped spinach on a plate and microwave on HIGH for 2 minutes.
▶ 2. Blend in a liquidiser to a smooth purée and keep aside.
▶ 3. Combine the oil, chopped onion, ginger and green chillies in a glass bowl and microwave on HIGH for 1 minute.

Facing page: **Top-** Vatana nu Oondhiyu, page 50
Bottom- Moong Dal Khandvi, page

▶ 4. Add the spinach purée, paneer, coriander powder,
turmeric powder, garam masala, cream and salt and
mix well. Microwave on HIGH for 3 minutes.

▶ **Serve hot.**

KHUMB KI SUBZI

Mushrooms cooked in a delectable spice
blend. Ideally accompanied with roti
or bread.

Prep. time :
5 min.
❖
Cooking time :
8 min.
❖
Serves 2.

2 cups mushrooms, cut into quarters
1 large tomato
1 onion, grated
2 teaspoons ginger-garlic paste
¼ teaspoon garam masala
½ teaspoon chilli powder
½ teaspoon coriander-cumin seed
(dhania-jeera) powder
½ teaspoon kasuri methi
(dried fenugreek leaves)
1 tablespoon cream
1 teaspoon oil
salt to taste

Facing page: Vegetable Makhanwala, page 38

For the garnish
2 tablespoons chopped coriander

▶ 1. Place the tomato on a shallow glass dish. Microwave on HIGH for 2 minutes.
▶ 2. Cool slightly, peel and purée in a liquidizer till smooth.
▶ 3. Combine the oil, grated onion and ginger-garlic paste in a glass bowl and microwave on HIGH for 1 minute.
▶ 4. Add the tomato purée and microwave on HIGH for 2 minutes.
▶ 5. Add all the other ingredients and mix well. Microwave on HIGH for 3 minutes.

▶ **Serve hot, garnished with the chopped coriander.**

VEGETABLE MAKHANWALA

Picture on page 36
Vegetables simmered in a rich tomato gravy.

Prep. time :
10 min.

❖

Cooking time :
14 min.

❖

Serves 4.

½ cup french beans,
cut into 25 mm. (1") pieces

½ cup carrots, cut into 25 (1") pieces

½ cup green peas

½ cup cauliflower florets

1 onion, sliced

¼ cup baby corn, sliced

38

12 mm. (½") piece ginger
3 cloves garlic
3 large tomatoes, sliced
¼ teaspoon turmeric (haldi) powder
1 teaspoon chilli powder
½ teaspoon cumin (jeera) seeds
1 teaspoon garam masala
4 tablespoons cream
½ teaspoon kasuri methi
(dried fenugreek leaves)
2 teaspoons sugar
4 tablespoons butter
salt to taste

For the garnish
1 tablespoon chopped coriander
1 teaspoon butter

1. Combine the onion, ginger, garlic, tomatoes, turmeric powder and chilli powder in a glass bowl. Microwave on HIGH for 4 minutes.
2. Blend this mixture in a liquidiser to get a smooth purée. Keep aside.
3. Put 2 tablespoons of butter and the cumin seeds in another glass bowl and microwave on HIGH for 1 minute.
4. Add the french beans, carrots, green peas, baby corn and cauliflower, cover with a lid and microwave on HIGH for 5 minutes. Keep aside.

5. In another glass bowl, add the remaining butter, cooked purée, vegetables, garam masala, cream, kasuri methi, sugar and salt and mix well. Microwave on HIGH for 4 minutes.

▶ Serve hot, garnished with the chopped coriander and butter.

PANEER IN QUICK WHITE GRAVY

Cottage cheese in a mildly spiced gravy.

Prep. time : 2 min.

❖

Cooking time : 5 min.

❖

Serves 2.

1 cup paneer, cut into 25 mm. (1") cubes
¼ teaspoon garam masala
¼ cup milk
2 tablespoons ghee
salt to taste

To be ground into an onion paste
1 large onion
1 tablespoon cashewnuts, chopped
4 cloves garlic
6 mm. (¼") piece ginger

For the garnish
2 tablespoons chopped coriander

1. Combine the ghee and the prepared onion paste in a glass bowl and microwave on HIGH for 2 minutes, stirring once in between after 1 minute.
2. Add the paneer, garam masala, milk, salt and 2 tablespoons of water and mix well.
3. Microwave on HIGH for a further 3 minutes.

▶ **Serve hot, garnished with the coriander.**

OONDHIYA

A classic Gujarati recipe adapted for the microwave. The colour of the vegetables is vibrant.

Prep. time :
40 min.
✤
Cooking time :
17 min.
✤
Serves 4.

250 grams Surti papdi
250 grams purple yam (kand)
100 grams yam (suran)
100 grams small potatoes
100 grams sweet potatoes (shakkariya)
100 grams small brinjals
1 to 2 bananas
1 tablespoon carom seeds (ajwain)
¼ teaspoon soda bi-carb
salt to taste

For the methi muthias
1 cup fenugreek
(methi) leaves, chopped

¼ cup whole wheat flour (gehun ka atta)

¼ cup Bengal gram flour (besan)

1 teaspoon green chilli-ginger paste

2 teaspoons sugar

juice of ½ lemon

¼ teaspoon garam masala

¼ teaspoon turmeric (haldi) powder

a pinch soda bi-carb

2 tablespoons oil

salt to taste

To be mixed into a masala

½ cup fresh coconut, grated

½ cup chopped coriander

¼ cup fresh green garlic, chopped

2 teaspoons coriander-cumin seed (dhania-jeera) powder

2 teaspoons green chilli-ginger paste

2 teaspoons chilli powder

2 teaspoons sugar

1 tablespoon lemon juice

salt to taste

For the tempering

¼ teaspoon asafoetida (hing)

6 tablespoons oil

For the methi muthias

▶ 1. Put the chopped fenugreek leaves in a bowl, add 1 teaspoon of salt and mix well.

2. Allow to stand for 5 to 7 minutes and squeeze out all the liquid from the leaves.

3. Combine the fenugreek with the remaining ingredients in a bowl and knead into a very soft dough by adding 3 tablespoons of water.

4. Spread this mixture onto a greased shallow glass dish and cover with a lid. Microwave on HIGH for 2 minutes.

5. Cool completely and cut into small squares.

How to proceed

1. String the Surti papdi, taking care not to separate the 2 sides.

2. Wash the papdi, add the carom seeds, soda bi-carb and salt and mix well.

3. Peel the purple yam, yam, potatoes and sweet potatoes and cut into big pieces.

4. Cut the brinjals and the banana into big pieces and cut a vertical slit in the centre of each piece.

5. Put the oil and asafoetida in a glass bowl and microwave on HIGH for 1 minute.

6. Add the Surti papdi, purple yam, yam, potatoes, sweet potatoes and brinjals and ¼ cup of water, cover with a lid and microwave on HIGH for 10 minutes, stirring once in between.

7. Add the prepared masala, bananas, methi muthias and mix well. Cover with a lid and microwave on HIGH for 4 minutes, stirring once in between.

▶ **Serve hot.**

Handy Tip :
Oondhiya is traditionally served with puris and shrikhand.

JEERA ALOO

Potatoes tossed with cumin seeds and spices.

Prep. time :
5 min.
✿
Cooking time :
7 min.
✿
Serves 2.

2 large potatoes, cut into fingers like french fries
1 teaspoon cumin (jeera) seeds
1 teaspoon chilli powder
¼ teaspoon turmeric (haldi) powder
2 teaspoons coriander (dhania) powder
2 tablespoons oil
salt to taste

For the garnish
2 tablespoons chopped coriander

▶ 1. In a glass bowl, add the oil and the cumin seeds and microwave on HIGH for 1 minute.

2. Add the rest of the ingredients, cover with a lid and microwave on HIGH for 6 minutes until the potatoes are soft.

▶ Serve hot, garnished with the chopped coriander.

PHOOLGOBHI AUR MUTTER KI KARI

Prep. time :
15 min.
❖
Cooking time :
11 min.
❖
Serves 4.

Picture on page 53
A coconut based curry gives this vegetable a delicious taste.

2 cups cauliflower, cut into small florets
1 cup green peas
2 bay leaves
4 tablespoons tomato purée
2 tablespoons fresh curds
½ teaspoon sugar
3 tablespoons oil
salt to taste

To be ground into a paste
1 onion
2 tablespoons fresh coconut, grated
2 cloves garlic
2 teaspoons coriander (dhania) seeds

45

1 teaspoon cumin (jeera) seeds
12 mm. (½") piece ginger
2 teaspoons poppy seeds (khus-khus)
4 whole red chillies

▶ 1. In a glass bowl, combine 2 tablespoons of oil and the cauliflower. Cover with a lid and microwave on HIGH for 4 minutes. Remove and keep aside.

▶ 2. In the same bowl, combine the green peas with 2 tablespoons of water and microwave on HIGH for 1 minute.

▶ 3. In another glass bowl, add the remaining 1 tablespoon of oil, the bay leaves and the prepared paste and microwave on HIGH for 2 minutes.

▶ 4. Add the tomato purée, curds, cauliflower, green peas, sugar, ½ cup of water and salt and microwave on HIGH for a further 4 minutes until the vegetables are soft.

▶ **Serve hot.**

Handy Tip :
Cut the cauliflower into uniform sized florets so that they cook evenly.

METHI MUTTER MALAI

A tasty combination of fenugreek leaves and green peas, enriched with cream, cashewnuts and poppy seeds.

Prep. time :
20 min.

❖

Cooking time :
7 min.

❖

Serves 2 to 3.

1½ cups chopped
fenugreek (methi) leaves
¼ teaspoon cumin (jeera) seeds
½ cup green peas
½ cup milk
3 tablespoons cream
a pinch sugar
2 tablespoons oil
salt to taste

To be ground into a paste
1 onion
1 green chilli
12 mm. (½") piece ginger
1 clove garlic
2 tablespoons cashewnuts
2 teaspoons poppy seeds (khus-khus)

1. Wash the fenugreek leaves, add ½ teaspoon of salt and leave aside for 10 minutes. Then, squeeze out the water.

In a glass bowl, combine 1 tablespoon of oil with the cumin seeds and fenugreek leaves and microwave on HIGH for 2 minutes. Remove and keep aside.

3. In another glass bowl, combine the green peas with 2 tablespoons of water and microwave on HIGH for 1 minute.

4. In a glass bowl, add the remaining 1 tablespoon of oil, the prepared paste and microwave on HIGH for 2 minutes.

5. Add the milk, cream, sugar, salt and the cooked fenugreek and peas and microwave on HIGH for another 2 minutes.

▶ **Serve hot.**

BATETA NU SHAAK

Potatoes cooked with tomato and Gujarati spices.

Prep. time :
10 min.
❖
Cooking time :
8 min.
❖
Serves 2.

1½ cups potatoes, peeled and cubed
½ teaspoon mustard (rai) seeds
½ teaspoon cumin (jeera) seeds
a pinch asafoetida (hing)
¼ teaspoon turmeric (haldi) powder
½ teaspoon chilli powder
1 small green chilli, finely chopped

6 mm. (¼") piece ginger, grated
½ tomato, finely chopped
1 tablespoon coriander-cumin seed
(dhania-jeera) powder

1 tablespoon sugar
2 tablespoons oil
salt to taste

For the garnish
2 tablespoons chopped coriander

1. Put the potato cubes in a glass bowl along with salt.
    Cover with a lid and microwave on HIGH for 4 minutes
    till they are cooked.
2. In another glass bowl, combine the oil, mustard
    seeds, cumin seeds, asafoetida, turmeric powder,
    chilli powder, green chilli and ginger and microwave
    on HIGH for 2 minutes.
3. Add the tomato and microwave on HIGH for 1 minute
    30 seconds.
4. Add the potatoes, coriander-cumin seed powder,
    sugar and salt, mix well and microwave on HIGH about
    30 seconds.
5. Garnish with the chopped coriander and serve hot.

Handy Tip :
You can also make the vegetable using boiled potatoes in
which case omit step no.1.

VATANA NU OONDHIYU

Picture on page 35

A quick way to make oondhiyu of fresh green peas, cooked with the pods.

Prep. time :
10 min.
❖
Cooking time :
4 min.
❖
Serves 2.

1 cup tender green peas (with pods)
2 pinches carom seeds (ajwain)
a pinch asafoetida (hing)
1 tablespoon oil
salt to taste

To be ground into a paste
2 green chillies
2 tablespoons chopped coriander
1 teaspoon lemon juice
2 tablespoons fresh green garlic, chopped
¼ teaspoon grated ginger

▶ 1. Wash and string the peas, taking care not to separate the segments.
▶ 2. Combine all the ingredients in a glass bowl and mix well.
▶ 3. Cover with a lid and microwave on HIGH for 4 minutes.
▶ 4. Remove from the microwave and allow it to rest for about 1 minute.

▶ **Serve hot.**

Handy Tips :

1. These peas have to be eaten in the same way as you would eat drumsticks.
2. If you do not wish to use fresh garlic, use 2 cloves of garlic and 1 tablespoon of chopped coriander instead.

KADAI PANEER

An all-time favourite recipe adapted for the microwave.

Prep. time :
20 min.

❧

Cooking time :
6 min.

❧

Serves 2.

1 cup paneer, cut into thick strips

1 large onion, finely chopped

2 cloves garlic, finely chopped

6 mm. (¼") piece ginger, grated

1 teaspoon coriander-cumin seed (dhania-jeera) powder

a pinch turmeric (haldi) powder

¾ teaspoon chilli powder

½ teaspoon garam masala

½ teaspoon kasuri methi (dried fenugreek leaves)

4 tablespoons tomato purée

¼ cup capsicum, sliced

1 tablespoon fresh cream

a pinch sugar

2 tablespoons oil

salt to taste

For the garnish
2 tablespoons chopped coriander

▶ 1. Combine the oil, onion, garlic and ginger in a glass bowl and microwave on HIGH for 2 minutes.
▶ 2. Add the coriander-cumin seed powder, turmeric powder, chilli powder, garam masala and kasuri methi and microwave on HIGH for 1 minute.
▶ 3. Add the tomato purée, capsicum and ¼ cup of water and microwave on HIGH for 2 minutes.
▶ 4. Add the paneer, cream, sugar, salt and ¼ cup of water and mix lightly. Microwave on HIGH for 1 minute.

▶ **Serve hot, garnished with the coriander.**

Handy Tips :
1. You can use 2 blanched and puréed tomatoes instead of 4 tablespoons of tomato purée and omit the water in step 3.
2. To blanch tomatoes, just microwave them on **HIGH** for 2 minutes, peel and purée them in a liquidizer.

Facing page: **Right-** Phoolgobhi aur Mutter ki Kari, page 45
Left- Khaman Chilli Pickle, page 76

KADDU KI SUBZI

A Rajasthani style red pumpkin vegetable.

1½ cups red pumpkin (kaddu), cubed
1 bay leaf
6 mm. (½") stick cinnamon
2 cloves
2 green cardamoms
½ teaspoon nigella seeds (kalonji)
¼ teaspoon mustard (rai) seeds
¼ teaspoon fenugreek (methi) seeds
a pinch asafoetida (hing)
¾ teaspoon chilli powder
1 teaspoon coriander-cumin seed
(dhania-jeera) powder
¼ teaspoon turmeric (haldi) powder
2 tablespoons finely chopped tomato
1 tablespoon fresh curds
½ teaspoon amchur
(dry mango powder)
½ teaspoon sugar
1 tablespoon ghee
salt to taste

Prep. time :
10 min.

✤

Cooking time :
8 min. 30 sec.

✤

Serves 2.

1. Combine the ghee, bay leaf, cinnamon, cloves, cardamoms, nigella seeds, mustard seeds, fenugreek seeds, asafoetida, chilli powder, coriander-cumin seed powder and turmeric powder in a shallow glass bowl and microwave on HIGH for 1 minute.

Facing page: Turai aur Narial, page 57

2. Add the chopped tomato and microwave on HIGH for 2 minutes.

3. Add the pumpkin cubes and salt, cover with a lid and microwave on HIGH for 5 minutes.

4. Allow to stand for 2 minutes and then add the curds, amchur powder and sugar and mix well. Microwave on HIGH for 30 seconds.

▶ **Serve hot with puris.**

SPICY CORN CURRY

Corn curry cooked using a South Indian spice blend. Serve with steamed rice.

Prep. time :
15 min.

❧

Cooking time :
12 min. 30 sec.

❧

Serves 4.

2 sweet corncobs, grated
½ cup potatoes, peeled and cubed
½ cup onions, cut into big pieces
1 tablespoon sambhar masala
½ tomato, chopped
1 teaspoon mustard (rai) seeds
10 curry leaves
a pinch asafoetida (hing)
2 tablespoons oil
salt to taste

For the garnish
2 tablespoons chopped coriander

1. Combine the oil, mustard seeds, curry leaves and asafoetida in a glass bowl and microwave on HIGH for 1½ minutes.
2. Add the potatoes , onions and 1½ cups of water and microwave on HIGH for 6 minutes.
3. Add the grated corn, sambhar masala, salt and 1 cup of water and microwave on HIGH for 3 minutes.
4. Add the tomato and microwave on HIGH for a further 2 minutes. Mix well.

▶ **Serve hot, garnished with the chopped coriander.**

TURAI AUR NARIAL

Picture on page 54

Ridge gourd and coconut are combined to make this scrumptious vegetable.

Prep. time :
10 min.
❖
Cooking time :
9 min.
❖
Serves 2.

2 cups turai (ridge gourd), thinly sliced
½ cup grated coconut
½ teaspoon mustard (rai) seeds
4 to 5 curry leaves
1 teaspoon ginger, grated
1 green chilli, finely chopped
1/8 teaspoon turmeric (haldi) powder
1 teaspoon sugar

juice of ½ lemon
1 tablespoon oil
salt to taste

For the garnish
2 tablespoons chopped coriander

1. In a glass bowl, combine the oil, mustard seeds, curry leaves, ginger and green chilli and microwave on HIGH for 1 minute.
2. Add the turai, turmeric powder and salt and mix well. Cover with a lid and microwave on HIGH for 6 minutes.
3. Add the coconut, sugar and lemon juice, cover with a lid and microwave on HIGH for 2 minutes.

▶ **Serve hot, garnished with the chopped coriander.**

Handy Tip :
Peel off only the hard veins of the turai taking care not to peel the turai completely.

DAL AUR CHAWAL

Try these lentil and rice preparations for a hassle-free, one dish meal. I would advise you to try the Masala Bhaat or Ek Toap Na Dal Bhaat if you prefer a little spice in your food. For those who favour milder flavours, try the Khumb Pulao or the cabbage rice and of course Fada ni Khichdi.

Its advisable, to soak the dal or rice for at least 15 minutes, so that cooking time is reduced.

HARIYALI DAL

A nutritious and tasty recipe using masoor dal and greens.

¾ cup uncooked split red lentils (masoor dal)

1 cup mixed greens
(palak, methi and coriander), chopped

1 small onion, chopped

2 cloves garlic, finely chopped

2 green chillies, finely chopped

6 mm. (¼") piece ginger, grated

½ teaspoon cumin (jeera) seeds

1 teaspoon amchur (dry mango powder)

1 medium tomato, chopped

¼ teaspoon turmeric (haldi) powder

¼ teaspoon chilli powder

2 tablespoons ghee

salt to taste

▶ 1. Clean and wash the dal. Allow it to soak in warm water for 30 minutes. Drain.

▶ 2. Combine the dal with 1½ cups of water in a glass bowl. Microwave on HIGH for 10 minutes, stirring twice in between after every 3 minutes.

▶ 3. Add an additional ½ cup of water, cover with a lid and microwave on HIGH for 3 minutes.

4. In another glass bowl, combine the ghee, onion, garlic, green chillies, ginger and cumin seeds and microwave on HIGH for 1 minute.

5. Add the cooked dal and the remaining ingredients, cover with a lid and microwave on HIGH for 4 minutes.

▶ **Serve hot.**

Handy Tip :
Use a large glass bowl, as the dal generally spills over when it is boiling.

EK TOAP NA DAL BHAAT

Picture on page 63

A speciality of Gujarat which makes a meal by itself.

Prep. time :
20 min.
❖
Cooking time :
18 min.
❖
Serves 4.

1 cup long grained rice
½ cup toovar (arhar) dal
2 to 3 pinches asafoetida (hing)
a pinch soda bi-carb
¼ teaspoon turmeric (haldi) powder
10 small onions
5 small potatoes
2 to 3 small brinjals
⅓ cup green peas
2 tablespoons ghee

To be mixed together into a masala

2 teaspoons coriander-cumin seed (dhania-jeera) powder

2 teaspoons sugar

1 teaspoon chilli powder

½ cup grated fresh coconut

4 to 5 tablespoons chopped coriander

a pinch asafoetida (hing)

salt to taste

For the garnish

2 tablespoons ghee

1. Make criss-cross slits on the onions, potatoes and brinjals, taking care not to separate the segments. Stuff the slits with the masala mixture. About half the mixture will remain.
2. Clean and wash the rice and dal separately.
3. Soak the dal in warm water for 30 minutes. Drain and keep aside.
4. Put the ghee, asafoetida, toovar dal, soda bi-carb and turmeric powder in a glass bowl and microwave on HIGH for 2 minutes.
5. Add the vegetables, rice, the remaining masala, salt with 3 cups of hot water and mix well. Microwave on HIGH for 16 minutes, stirring twice in between after every 5 to 6 minutes.
6. Pour some ghee over the dish and serve hot with buttermilk.

Facing page: Ek Toap Na Dal Bhaat, page 61

CABBAGE RICE

A delicately flavoured rice dish.

Prep. time :
10 min.

♣

Cooking time :
15 min.

♣

Serves 4.

1 cup long grained rice
1 onion, grated
½ cup shredded cabbage
1 capsicum, sliced
1 teaspoon pepper powder
½ cup grated cheese
2 tablespoons butter
salt to taste

▶ 1. Clean and wash the rice. Soak in warm water for about 10 minutes. Drain and keep aside.

▶ 2. Combine the grated onion and butter in a glass bowl and microwave on HIGH for 2 minutes.

▶ 3. Add the rice, 2 cups of hot water and salt and microwave on HIGH for 10 minutes. stirring twice in between after every 3 to 4 minutes.

▶ 4. Add the cabbage, capsicum, pepper powder and half of the cheese and mix well.

▶ 5. Microwave on HIGH for 3 minutes. Allow it to stand for 3 minutes.

▶ 6. Serve hot garnished with the remaining cheese.

Facing page: **Top-** Gajar ka Halwa, page 78
Bottom- Meetha Chawal, page 81

FADA NI KHICHADI

A traditional Gujarati preparation made of broken wheat. A meal by itself.

Prep. time :
10 min.

❖

Cooking time :
13 min.

❖

Serves 4.

1 cup broken wheat (dalia),
cleaned and washed

1 teaspoon cumin (jeera) seeds

¼ teaspoon asafoetida (hing)

2 cloves

12 mm. (½") piece cinnamon

½ cup onion, diced

½ cup french beans, diced

½ cup carrots, diced

½ cup cauliflower, cut into florets

¼ cup green peas

½ teaspoon green chilli-ginger paste

2 teaspoons chilli powder

½ teaspoon turmeric (haldi) powder

2 tablespoons ghee

salt to taste

For the garnish

2 tablespoons ghee

2 tablespoons chopped coriander

▶ 1. In a glass bowl, combine the ghee, cumin seeds, asafoetida, cloves and cinnamon and microwave on HIGH for 1 minute.

2. Add the broken wheat, mix well and cover with a lid. Microwave on HIGH for 1 minute, stirring once in between after 30 seconds.
3. Add all the other ingredients and 2 cups of hot water and mix well.
4. Cover with a lid and microwave on HIGH for 9 minutes.
5. Stir well and microwave on HIGH for 2 more minutes.
6. Pour the ghee over the dish and serve hot, garnished with the coriander.

Handy Tip :

This dish tastes great with curds and pickle.
Broken wheat is also called "Bulgur" wheat.

SPICY PULAO

Rice and vegetable flavoured with a spicy red chilli paste. A fiery feast.

Prep. time :
10 min.

❖

Cooking time :
13 min.

❖

Serves 4.

1 cup long grained rice
½ cup green peas
½ cup carrots, diced
2 tablespoons curds
a few mint leaves
2 tablespoons ghee
salt to taste

To be ground into a chilli paste
6 Kashmiri chillies
3 cloves garlic

12 mm. (½") piece ginger
2 teaspoons coriander-cumin seed
(dhania-jeera) powder

▶ 1. Clean and wash the rice. Soak in warm water for about 10 minutes. Drain and keep aside.

▶ 2. In a glass bowl, combine the ghee and the chilli paste and microwave on HIGH for 1 minute.

▶ 3. Add the rice, peas, carrots, curds and salt with 2½ cups of hot water. Microwave on HIGH for 12 minutes, stirring twice in between after every 4 minutes.

▶ 4. Add the mint leaves and toss lightly.

▶ **Serve hot.**

MASALA BHAAT

This Maharashtrian recipe of rice, tendli and peas, simmered with spices makes a great meal by itself.

Prep. time :
15 min.
❖
Cooking time :
15 min.
❖
Serves 4.

1 cup long grained rice
1 cup tendli, slice horizontally
½ cup green peas
½ teaspoon mustard (rai) seeds
½ teaspoon cumin (jeera) seeds
3 green cardamoms
12 mm. (½") piece cinnamon
5 cloves

¼ teaspoon fenugreek (methi) seeds
2 green chillies
5 curry leaves
¼ teaspoon asafoetida (hing)
½ teaspoon turmeric (haldi) powder
½ cup grated fresh coconut
¼ cup chopped coriander
8 to 10 nos. cashewnuts, fried
1 tablespoon ghee
salt to taste

For the spice powder
2 cloves
12 mm. (½") piece cinnamon
1 teaspoon coriander (dhania) seeds
1 teaspoon cumin (jeera) seeds
½ cup grated dry coconut (kopra)
2 tablespoons sesame (til) seeds

For the spice powder
1. Combine all the ingredients in a glass plate and microwave on HIGH for 2 minutes.
2. Grind to a fine powder in a food processor. Keep aside.

How to proceed
1. Clean and wash the rice. Soak in warm water for about 10 minutes. Drain and keep aside.
2. Combine the mustard seeds, cumin seeds, cardamoms, cinnamon, cloves, fenugreek seeds,

69

green chillies, curry leaves, asafoetida and ghee in a glass bowl and microwave on HIGH for 1 minute.

3. Add the rice, tendli, peas, turmeric powder, spice powder and salt and mix well. Microwave on HIGH for 2 minutes.

4. Add 2½ cups of hot water to the rice mixture, mix well and microwave on HIGH for 10 minutes, stirring once in between after 5 minutes.

5. Add the coconut, coriander and cashewnuts and mix well.

▶ Serve hot.

KHUMB PULAO

A delicious combination of rice with fresh green onions and mushrooms.

Prep. time :
10 min.
❖
Cooking time :
14 min.
❖
Serves 4.

1 cup long grained rice
1 cup mushrooms, sliced
4 spring onions
2 cloves
12 mm. (½") piece cinnamon
2 green cardamoms
1 bay leaf
1 teaspoon garam masala
1 teaspoon cumin (jeera) powder
2 tablespoons oil
salt to taste

1. Clean and wash the rice. Soak in warm water for about 10 minutes. Drain and keep aside.
2. Chop the spring onion whites and the greens separately. Keep aside.
3. Combine the oil, spring onion whites, cloves, cinnamon, cardamoms and bay leaf in a glass bowl. Microwave on HIGH for 2 minutes.
4. Add the mushrooms and microwave on HIGH for 1 more minute.
5. Add the rice, mix well and microwave on HIGH for 1 minute.
6. Add 2 cups of hot water to the rice mixture along with the spring onion greens and salt and mix well. Microwave on HIGH for 10 minutes, stirring twice in between after every 4 minutes.

▶ **Serve hot.**

PANEER PULAO

Tangy tomato and paneer pulao.

1 cup long grained rice
1 onion, sliced
2 tablespoons ginger-garlic paste
1 green chilli, chopped
1/3 cup tomato purée
1/2 teaspoon garam masala
1/2 teaspoon chilli powder
1 capsicum, sliced
1 cup paneer, cubed
2 tablespoons chopped coriander
2 tablespoons oil
salt to taste

Prep. time :
10 min.
❖
Cooking time :
13 min.
❖
Serves 2.

▶ 1. Clean and wash the rice. Soak in warm water for about 10 minutes. Drain and keep aside.

▶ 2. Combine the oil, onion, ginger-garlic paste and green chilli in a glass bowl. Microwave on HIGH for 2 minutes.

▶ 3. Add the tomato purée, garam masala, chilli powder, capsicum, salt and rice and mix well. Microwave on HIGH for 1 minute.

▶ 4. Add the paneer, 2 cups of hot water and coriander to the rice and mix well. Microwave on HIGH for 10 minutes, stirring twice in between after every 4 minutes.

▶ Serve hot.

CHATPATE ACHAAR

These quick pickles add the much needed spice to your meal.

QUICK CARROT PICKLE

Carrot and capsicum tossed with mustard and spices with a pungent flavouring of mustard oil.

Prep. time :
10 min.

❖

Cooking time :
2 min. 30 sec.

❖

Makes 2 cups.

1½ cups carrots, cut into strips
1 cup capsicum, cut into strips
4 tablespoons mustard oil

To be combined into a masala mixture

½ tablespoon nigella seeds (kalonji)

2 tablespoons split yellow mustard seeds (rai na kuria)

¼ teaspoon asafoetida (hing)

1 tablespoon chilli powder

½ teaspoon fenugreek seeds (methi) powder

1 tablespoon salt

1. Combine the masala mixture, carrots and capsicum in a bowl and mix well.
2. In another bowl, microwave the mustard oil on HIGH for 2 minutes till it is hot.

3. Pour the hot oil over the carrot and capsicum and mix again.
4. Cover and microwave on HIGH for 30 seconds.
5. Cool and store refrigerated for upto 3 days.

Handy Tip :
You can use refined oil instead of mustard oil if you prefer.

KHAMAN CHILLI PICKLE

Picture on page 53

Dhokla and chillies cooked together to get the scrumptious accompaniment.

Picture on page 53

Prep. time :
10 min.

♣

Cooking time :
5 min.

♣

Serves 4.

1 recipe khaman dhokla, page 30
6 big green chillies (Bhavnagri chillies)
2 tablespoons mustard (rai) seeds
2 tablespoons sesame (til) seeds
¼ teaspoon asafoetida (hing)
¼ teaspoon black salt (sanchal)
1 teaspoon amchur (dry mango powder)
2 tablespoons oil
salt to taste

1. Prepare the khaman dhokla as mentioned in the recipe on page 30. Crumble the dhokla and keep aside.

2. Slice the chillies. Keep aside.

3. In a glass bowl, combine the oil, mustard seeds, sesame seeds and asafoetida and microwave on HIGH for 2 minutes.

4. Add the green chillies, black salt, amchur powder and salt and microwave on HIGH for 2 minutes.

5. Add the crumbled dhokla and 2 tablespoons of water and microwave on HIGH for 1 minute.

▶ Serve warm.

DESI MITHAI

Traditional desserts like Gajar ka Halwa, Gol Papdi, Kaju Kopra Sheera etc. can be made in minutes thanks to the microwave. The microwave has one more advantage. When making milk based desserts like phirni, the milk never gets scorched!

GAJAR KA HALWA

Picture on page 64
A quick and easy version.

2 cups grated carrots
¼ cup milk powder
5 tablespoons sugar
¼ teaspoon cardamom (elaichi) powder
1 tablespoon melted ghee

For the garnish
1 tablespoon sliced pistachios
and cashewnuts

1 edible silver leaf (varq)

Prep. time :
5 min.
❖
Cooking time :
6 min.
❖
Serves 2.

▶ 1. In a glass bowl, combine the ghee and grated carrots. Cover with a lid and microwave on HIGH for 4 minutes.

▶ 2. Add the milk powder, sugar, cardamom powder and mix well. Cover with a lid and microwave on HIGH for 2 minutes.

▶ Serve hot, garnished with the sliced pistachios, cashewnuts and varq.

GOL PAPDI

A wheat flour sweet which is easy to prepare.

Prep. time :
5 min.

❖

Cooking time :
3 min. 30 sec.

❖

Makes 20 pieces.

½ cup whole wheat flour (gehun ka atta)
⅓ cup jaggery (gur), grated
½ teaspoon poppy seeds (khus-khus)
¼ teaspoon cardamom (elaichi) powder
4 tablespoons melted ghee

1. Sprinkle the poppy seeds on a 100 mm. (4") diameter greased thali. Keep aside.

2. Combine the ghee and wheat flour in a glass bowl and microwave on HIGH for 3 minutes 30 seconds, till it turns golden brown in colour. Mix well.

3. Remove from the microwave and add the jaggery and cardamom powder while the mixture is hot. Stir well till the jaggery melts.

4. Pour the mixture into the greased thali with poppy seeds while still warm and spread it evenly with the help of the base of a small bowl (katori).

5. Cut into diamond shapes while still warm.

6. Store in an air-tight container when cool.

Handy Tip :
You can add 1 tablespoon of milk along with the jaggery if the mixture becomes too hard.

SITAFAL FIRNI

Milk thickened with rice flour and flavoured with custard apple.

Prep. time :
5 min.
✤
Cooking time :
6 min.
✤
Serves 2.

1½ cups full fat milk
2 tablespoons long grained rice
4 tablespoons powdered sugar
¼ teaspoon cardamom (elaichi) powder
¾ cup custard apple
(sitafal) pulp, deseeded

▶ 1. Grind the rice to a fine powder in a food processor.

▶ 2. In a large glass bowl, combine 1 cup of milk and the ground rice, mix well and microwave on HIGH for 4 minutes, stirring twice in between after 2 minutes.

▶ 3. Add the remaining milk and microwave on HIGH for a further 2 minutes.

▶ 4. Remove and allow to cool. Add the sugar, cardamom powder and custard apple pulp and mix well.

▶ 5. Chill for 2 to 3 hours.

▶ **Serve chilled.**

Handy Tip :
You can add another fruit of your choice instead of the custard apple eg, strawberry , mango etc.

MEETHA CHAWAL

Picture on page 64

Delicious saffron and cardamom flavoured sweet rice.

Prep. time :
10 min.

❖

Cooking time :
21 min.

❖

Serves 4.

1 cup uncooked rice
25 mm. (1") stick cinnamon
2 cloves
3 green cardamoms
a few saffron strands
1 cup sugar
2 tablespoons ghee

For the garnish

a few blanched and sliced almonds and pistachios

1. Wash the rice and soak in warm water for 10 to 15 minutes. Drain and keep aside.
2. In a glass bowl, combine the ghee, rice, cinnamon, cloves and cardamoms and microwave on HIGH for 1 minute.
3. Add the saffron, 2½ cups of hot water and mix well. Microwave on HIGH for 18 minutes, stirring thrice in between after every 5 minutes.
4. Add the sugar and mix well . Microwave on HIGH for a further 2 minutes until the sugar dissolves.

▶ **Serve hot, garnished with almonds and pistachios.**

KAJU KOPRA SHEERA

A dessert of cashewnuts and fresh coconut flavoured with cardamom and saffron.

Prep. time :
10 min.
❖
Cooking time :
4 min.
❖
Serves 2.

½ cup (50 grams) cashewnuts, coarsely powdered

½ cup grated fresh coconut

⅓ cup sugar

a pinch of cardamom (elaichi) powder

a few drops of saffron food colour

2 tablespoons ghee

▶ 1. Combine the cashewnut powder, grated coconut and ghee in a glass bowl and microwave on HIGH for 2 minutes, stirring once in between.

▶ 2. Add the sugar, cardamom powder, saffron food colour and ¼ cup of water and mix well. Microwave on HIGH for 2 minutes, stirring once in between.

▶ **Serve warm.**

ATTA KA SHEERA

Wheat flour halwa which is delicious and yet easy to make.

Prep. time :
5 min.
❖
Cooking time :
5 min.
❖
Serves 4.

½ cup whole wheat flour (gehun ka atta)
½ cup sugar
½ teaspoon cardamom (elaichi) powder
¼ cup melted ghee

For the garnish
sliced almonds

1. In a glass bowl, combine the wheat flour and ghee and mix well. Microwave on HIGH for 3 minutes. Mix well.

2. Add the sugar, cardamom powder and ¾ cup of water and microwave on HIGH for 2 minutes until the sugar has dissolved. Mix well.

Serve hot.

SOOJI KA HALWA

A creamy halwa that has a special touch.

$^1/_3$ cup semolina (sooji/rawa)
$^1/_3$ cup milk
6 tablespoons sugar
3 tablespoons ghee
$^1/_4$ teaspoon cardamom (elaichi) powder
1 ripe banana ,finely chopped

Cooking time :
9 min. 45 sec.
❖
Serves 4.

1. Put the milk, sugar and $1^1/_2$ teacups of water in a large glass bowl and microwave on HIGH for about 5 minutes, stirring once in between after $2^1/_2$ minutes. Keep aside.

2. Put the ghee in another glass bowl and microwave on HIGH for about 15 seconds.

3. Add the semolina, mix well and microwave on HIGH for 3 minutes, stirring in-between after every 1 minute or until the semolina is light pink in colour.

4. Add the parboiled sweetened milk mixture and banana and mix well. Microwave on HIGH for $1^1/_2$ minutes, stirring in-between after every 30 seconds.

5. Sprinkle cardamom powder on top.

▶ **Serve hot.**

500 Flour
250 Rawa
125 Bull

4 Rice
1 Dal
½ af seed 1 Tb so
while fi

Dal

Boil dal, Haldi, हींग.
In the pan Heat oil put mustard, curry
patta, onion, tomato any vegetable, lady finger
drum stick, tamrind water [put int
cookes and one steam.

samber powder

Dhania   50 gm ⎫
chana dal   1 Tb   ⎪ Roast
tuwar "   1 Tb   ⎬ and mixiy
मिली जीरा   ⎪
जीरा   -   1 tb   ⎪
Red chillie 10   ⎭

Coconut   1 glass
quater glass Roasted chan
green chillie
ginger, garlic

Chunty
Frost tomato or fresh - 4
foue Tb coconut
: white dal   2 Tb
Red chillie   4
Tamrind

Chillie powder
garlic   2 pod

Fry except
coconut cool th
and put in the
mixiy add